ILLUSTRATED REMINDERS
of GOD'S GRACE

WORKMAN PUBLISHING • NEW YORK

Library of Congress Cataloging-in-Publication Data is available

ISBN 978-1-5235-0117-5

Design by Janet Vicario

Cover illustration by Home Again Creative
Text selections by Liz Davis

Workman books are available at special discounts when purchased in bulk for premiums and sales promotions as well as for fund-raising or educational use. Special editions or book excerpts can also be created to specification. For details, contact the Special Sales Director at the address below, or send an email to specialmarkets@workman.com.

Workman Publishing Co., Inc.
225 Varick Street
New York, NY 10014-4381
workman.com

WORKMAN is a registered trademark of Workman Publishing Co., Inc.

Printed in China

First printing August 2017

10 9 8 7 6 5 4 3

With gratitude and admiration for the leaders of
Lamplighters Bible Study of Covenant Presbyterian Church
in Austin, Texas

GALATIANS 3:26–29

26 For you are all children of God, through faith in Christ Jesus.

27 For as many of you as were baptized into Christ have put on Christ.

28 There is neither Jew nor Greek, there is neither slave nor free man, there is neither male nor female; for you are all one in Christ Jesus.

29 If you are Christ's, then you are Abraham's offspring and heirs according to promise.

World English Bible

YOU
ARE A
CHILD
of
GOD

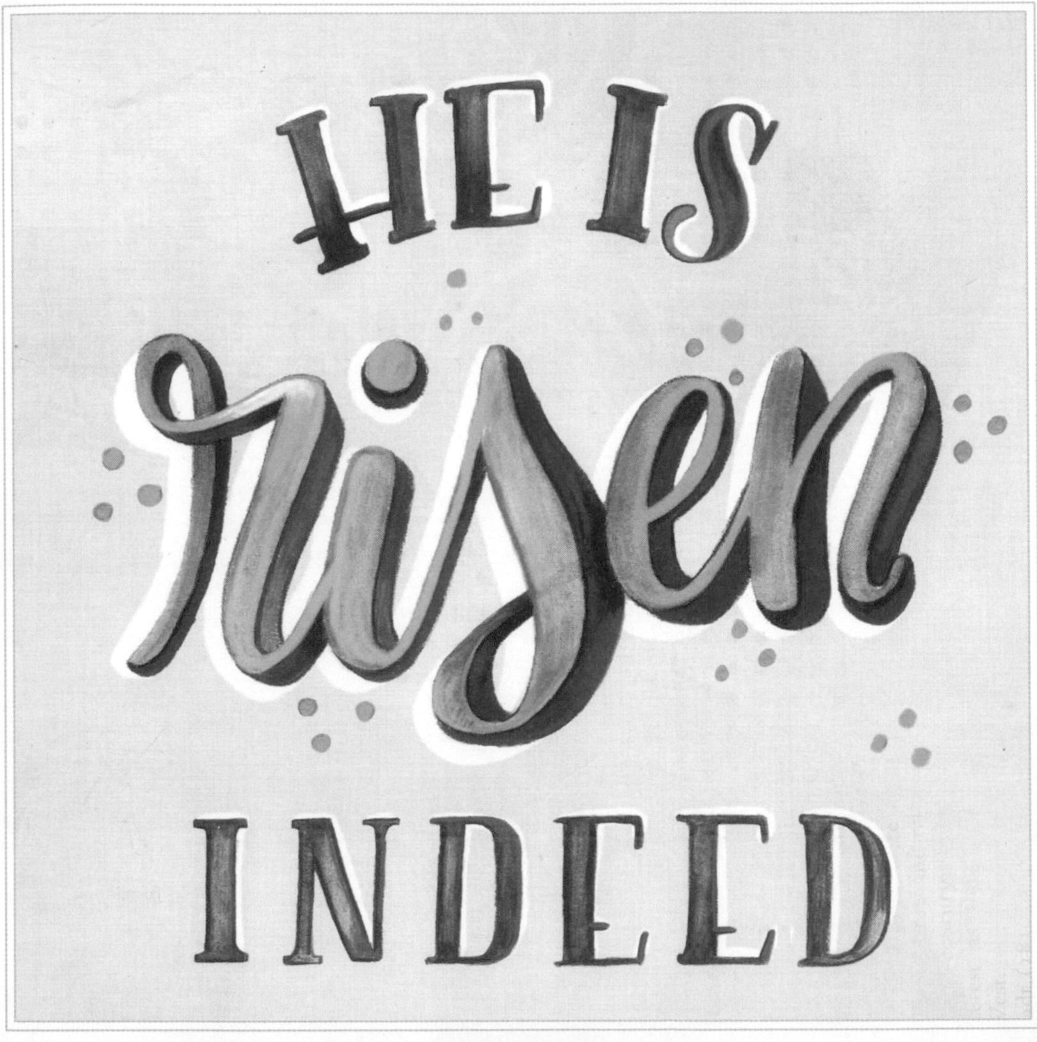

HE IS

risen

INDEED

1 JOHN 2:24–25

24 As for you, see that what you have heard from the beginning remains in you. If it does, you also will remain in the Son and in the Father.

25 And this is what he promised us—eternal life.

New International Version

Mark 11:7–11

7 And they bring the colt unto Jesus, and cast on him their garments; and he sat upon him.

8 And many spread their garments upon the way; and others branches, which they had cut from the fields.

9 And they that went before, and they that followed, cried, Hosanna; Blessed *is* he that cometh in the name of the Lord:

10 Blessed *is* the kingdom that cometh, *the kingdom* of our father David: Hosanna in the highest.

11 And he entered into Jerusalem, into the temple; and when he had looked round about upon all things, it being now eventide, he went out unto Bethany with the twelve.

American Standard Version

Blessed IS HE Who Comes IN THE NAME OF THE Lord

AS FOR ME & MY HOUSE,

WE WILL SERVE THE LORD.

JOSHUA 24:15 (KJV)

We must imitate his life
and his ways if we are to be

TRULY
ENLIGHTENED

and set free from the darkness
of our own hearts.

—THOMAS À KEMPIS

Philippians 4:8–9

8 Finally, brothers, whatever things are true, whatever things are honorable, whatever things are just, whatever things are pure, whatever things are lovely, whatever things are of good report; if there is any virtue, and if there is any praise, think about these things.

9 The things which you learned, received, heard, and saw in me: do these things, and the God of peace will be with you.

World English Bible

Be Thou my Vision, O Lord of my heart;
Naught be all else to me, save that Thou art:
Thou my best Thought, by day or by night,
Waking or sleeping, Thy presence my light.

Be Thou my Wisdom, and Thou my true Word;
I ever with Thee and Thou with me, Lord.
Thou my great Father, I Thy true son;
Thou in me dwelling, and I with Thee one.

Riches I heed not, nor man's empty praise,
Thou mine Inheritance, now and always:
Thou and Thou only, first in my heart,
High King of Heaven, my Treasure Thou art.

High King of Heaven, my victory won,
May I reach Heaven's joys, O bright Heav'n's Sun!
Heart of my own heart, whate'er befall,
Still be my Vision, O Ruler of all.

translated by Mary Elizabeth Byrne

BE THOU
MY
VISION
O LORD
OF MY
HEART

WHAT A FRIEND WE HAVE IN JESUS.

John 15:15–17

15 No longer do I call you servants, for a servant does not know what his master is doing; but I have called you friends, for all things that I heard from My Father I have made known to you.
16 You did not choose Me, but I chose you and appointed you that you should go and bear fruit, and that your fruit should remain, that whatever you ask the Father in My name He may give you.
17 These things I command you, that you love one another.

New King James Version

Lift every voice and

Till earth

RING with

of LIBERTY.

and SING,
heaven ring,
the harmonies

—James Weldon Johnson

Nehemiah 9:6

You alone are the Lord.
You have made the heavens,
The heaven of heavens with all their host,
The earth and all that is on it,
The seas and all that is in them.
You give life to all of them
And the heavenly host bows down before You.

New American Standard Bible

Oh LORD who
BLESSED
the LOAVES and FISHES
BLESS the FOOD
upon these dishes
And as the SUGAR in the TEA,
Let US LORD be
STIRRED
to thee.

JESUS CHRIST
is the
FIRST and the LAST,
THE BEGINNING
and
THE END.

Revelation 22:12–14

12 Behold, I come quickly; and my reward is with me, to render to each man according as his work is.
13 I am the Alpha and the Omega, the first and the last, the beginning and the end.
14 Blessed are they that wash their robes, that they may have the right to come to the tree of life, and may enter in by the gates into the city.

American Standard Version

Isaiah 46:3–4

3 Listen to me, you descendants of Jacob,
    all the remnant of the people of Israel,
you whom I have upheld since your birth,
    and have carried since you were born.
4 Even to your old age and gray hairs
    I am he, I am he who will sustain you.
I have made you and I will carry you;
    I will sustain you and I will rescue you.

New International Version

There are no "ifs"
in God's kingdom...
His timing is
perfect.

~ CORRIE TEN BOOM ~

GOD NEVER SAID

the Journey WOULD BE

EASY

But

HE DID SAY

the Arrival WOULD BE

WORTHWHILE

Max Lucado

THANKS BE to GOD
for HIS
INDESCRIBABLE
GIFT

2 Corinthians 9:10–15

10 For God is the one who provides seed for the farmer and then bread to eat. In the same way, he will provide and increase your resources and then produce a great harvest of generosity in you.

11 Yes, you will be enriched in every way so that you can always be generous. And when we take your gifts to those who need them, they will thank God.
12 So two good things will result from this ministry of giving—the needs of the believers in Jerusalem will be met, and they will joyfully express their thanks to God.

13 As a result of your ministry, they will give glory to God. For your generosity to them and to all believers will prove that you are obedient to the Good News of Christ.
14 And they will pray for you with deep affection because of the overflowing grace God has given to you.
15 Thank God for this gift too wonderful for words!

New Living Translation

Numbers 6:22–27

22 And the Lord spake unto Moses, saying,

23 Speak unto Aaron and unto his sons, saying, On this wise ye shall bless the children of Israel, saying unto them,

24 The Lord bless thee, and keep thee:

25 The Lord make his face shine upon thee, and be gracious unto thee:

26 The Lord lift up his countenance upon thee, and give thee peace.

27 And they shall put my name upon the children of Israel, and I will bless them.

King James Version

THE LORD BLESS YOU AND KEEP YOU;
THE LORD MAKE HIS FACE SHINE UPON YOU,

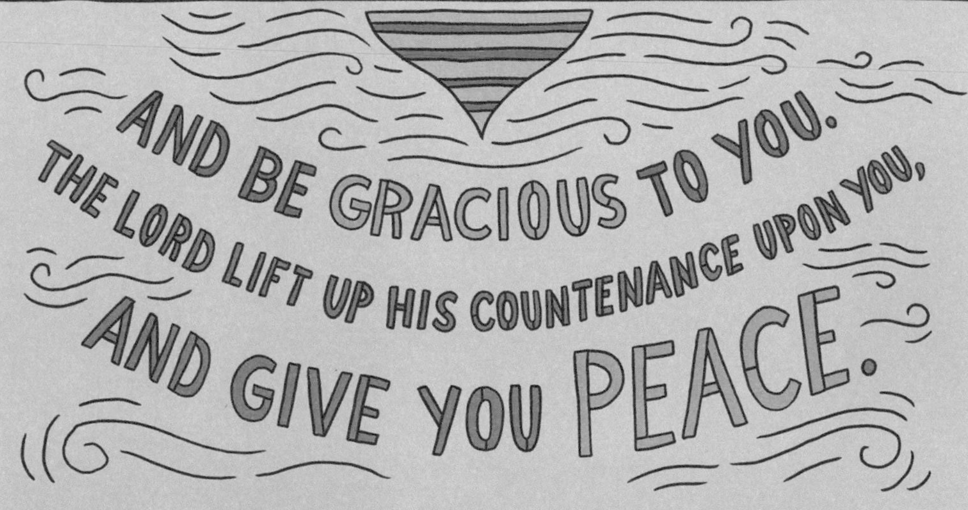

ALL THY WORKS
SHALL PRAISE THY NAME IN
EARTH AND SKY
AND
SEA

Holy, holy, holy! Lord God Almighty!
Early in the morning our song shall rise to thee.
Holy, holy, holy! Merciful and mighty,
God in three persons, blessed Trinity!

Holy, holy, holy! All the saints adore thee,
casting down their golden crowns around the glassy sea;
cherubim and seraphim falling down before thee,
which wert, and art, and evermore shalt be.

Holy, holy, holy! Though the darkness hide thee,
though the eye of sinful man thy glory may not see,
only thou art holy; there is none beside thee,
perfect in power, in love and purity.

Holy, holy, holy! Lord God Almighty!
All thy works shall praise thy name, in earth and sky and sea.
Holy, holy, holy! Merciful and mighty,
God in three persons, blessed Trinity.

Reginald Heber

THOU CHANGEST not,

AS THOU HAST

THOU F

THOMAS CHISHOLM

THY COMPASSIONS, THEY FAIL NOT,

BEEN,

orever

WILT BE.

JOHN 14:27

Peace I leave with you. My peace I give to you; not as the world gives, give I to you. Don't let your heart be troubled, neither let it be fearful.

World English Bible

I know the
PEACE-
SPEAKER.
I know
HIM
by name.

LET US GO FORTH

TO

SERVE THE

WORLD

AS

THOSE WHO

LOVE OUR LORD

& SAVIOR

JESUS CHRIST

Romans 12:9–16

9 Don't just pretend to love others. Really love them. Hate what is wrong. Hold tightly to what is good.
10 Love each other with genuine affection, and take delight in honoring each other.
11 Never be lazy, but work hard and serve the Lord enthusiastically.
12 Rejoice in our confident hope. Be patient in trouble, and keep on praying.
13 When God's people are in need, be ready to help them. Always be eager to practice hospitality.

14 Bless those who persecute you. Don't curse them; pray that God will bless them.
15 Be happy with those who are happy, and weep with those who weep.
16 Live in harmony with each other. Don't be too proud to enjoy the company of ordinary people. And don't think you know it all!

New Living Translation

Matthew 18:18–20

18 Most certainly I tell you, whatever things you bind on earth will have been bound in heaven, and whatever things you release on earth will have been released in heaven.

19 Again, assuredly I tell you, that if two of you will agree on earth concerning anything that they will ask, it will be done for them by my Father who is in heaven.

20 For where two or three are gathered together in my name, there I am in the middle of them.

World English Bible

WE GATHER together TO ASK THE Lord's BLESSING

Pray

without ceasing

1 THESSALONIANS 5:17 KJV

For as the heavens are
higher than the earth,
so are God's ways higher
than our ways and God's thoughts
than our thoughts.

Isaiah 55:8–9

8 For my thoughts are not your thoughts, neither are your ways my ways, saith the Lord.

9 For as the heavens are higher than the earth, so are my ways higher than your ways, and my thoughts than your thoughts.

King James Version

2 Corinthians 7:10

For the kind of sorrow God wants us to experience leads us away from sin and results in salvation. There's no regret for that kind of sorrow. But worldly sorrow, which lacks repentance, results in spiritual death.

New Living Translation

Affliction is able to drown out EVERY EARTHLY VOICE... but the voice of eternity within a man IT CANNOT DROWN.

~Søren Kierkegaard

COME
LORD JESUS
BE OUR GUEST
AND LET THESE
GIFTS TO US BE
BLESSED

Revelation 3:20–22

20 Behold, I stand at the door and knock. If anyone hears my voice and opens the door, then I will come in to him, and will dine with him, and he with me.
21 He who overcomes, I will give to him to sit down with me on my throne, as I also overcame, and sat down with my Father on his throne.
22 He who has an ear, let him hear what the Spirit says to the assemblies.

World English Bible

As far as THE EAST is from THE WEST

so far HATH
HE
REMOVED
our
transgressions
FROM us

PSALM 103:12 (KJV)

All hail the pow'r of Jesus' name!
Let angels prostrate fall.
Bring forth the royal diadem,
And crown Him Lord of all.
Bring forth the royal diadem,
And crown Him Lord of all.

Let ev'ry kindred, ev'ry tribe,
On this terrestrial ball,
To him all majesty ascribe,
And crown him Lord of all.
To him all majesty ascribe,
And crown him Lord of all.

Edward Perronet

WE'LL JOIN THE EVERLASTING SONG AND CROWN HIM LORD of ALL.

Amazing Grace
HOW SWEET THE SOUND

Amazing grace! how sweet the sound,
that saved a wretch like me!
I once was lost but now am found,
was blind but now I see.

'Twas grace that taught my heart to fear,
and grace my fears relieved;
how precious did that grace appear
the hour I first believed!

The Lord has promised good to me,
his word my hope secures;
he will my shield and portion be
as long as life endures.

Through many dangers, toils, and snares,
I have already come;
'tis grace hath brought me safe thus far,
and grace will lead me home.

When we've been there ten thousand years,
bright shining as the sun,
we've no less days to sing God's praise
than when we'd first begun.

John Newton

O God, make the door of this house wide enough to receive all who need human love and fellowship, narrow enough to shut out all envy, pride, and strife. Make its threshold smooth enough to be no stumbling block to children, nor to straying feet, but rugged and strong enough to turn back the tempter's power. **God, make the door of this house the gateway to Thine eternal Kingdom.**

Thomas Ken

God, make the DOOR of this HOUSE the gateway to Thine eternal KINGDOM

make A joyful noise!!

You are good & all-powerful,
CARING for each one of us
as though the only one in your care,
and yet for ALL as
for each individual.

—ST. AUGUSTINE

Psalm 147:1–7

1 Praise ye the Lord: for it is good to sing praises unto our God; for it is pleasant; and praise is comely.

2 The Lord doth build up Jerusalem: he gathereth together the outcasts of Israel.

3 He healeth the broken in heart, and bindeth up their wounds.

4 He telleth the number of the stars; he calleth them all by their names.

5 Great is our Lord, and of great power: his understanding is infinite.

6 The Lord lifteth up the meek: he casteth the wicked down to the ground.

7 Sing unto the Lord with thanksgiving; sing praise upon the harp unto our God.

King James Version

Colossians 3:12–17

12 So, as those who have been chosen of God, holy and beloved, put on a heart of compassion, kindness, humility, gentleness and patience;

13 bearing with one another, and forgiving each other, whoever has a complaint against anyone; just as the Lord forgave you, so also should you.

14 Beyond all these things *put on* love, which is the perfect bond of unity.

15 Let the peace of Christ rule in your hearts, to which indeed you were called in one body; and be thankful.

16 Let the word of Christ richly dwell within you, with all wisdom teaching and admonishing one another with psalms *and* hymns *and* spiritual songs, singing with thankfulness in your hearts to God.

17 Whatever you do in word or deed, *do* all in the name of the Lord Jesus, giving thanks through Him to God the Father.

New American Standard Bible

BEGIN EACH DAY WITH A GRATEFUL HEART.

Evening is here,
the board is spread,
Thanks be to God
who gives us
bread!

JOHN 6:32–35

32 Then Jesus said to them, "Very truly, I tell you, it was not Moses who gave you the bread from heaven, but it is my Father who gives you the true bread from heaven.
33 For the bread of God is that which comes down from heaven and gives life to the world."
34 They said to him, "Sir, give us this bread always."

35 Jesus said to them, "I am the bread of life. Whoever comes to me will never be hungry, and whoever believes in me will never be thirsty."

New Revised Standard Version

Speak
THE
TRUTH

In
LOVE

Psalm 121:1–8

1 I will lift up mine eyes unto the hills, from whence cometh my help.

2 My help cometh from the Lord, which made heaven and earth.

3 He will not suffer thy foot to be moved: he that keepeth thee will not slumber.

4 Behold, he that keepeth Israel shall neither slumber nor sleep.

5 The Lord is thy keeper: the Lord is thy shade upon thy right hand.

6 The sun shall not smite thee by day, nor the moon by night.

7 The Lord shall preserve thee from all evil: he shall preserve thy soul.

8 The Lord shall preserve thy going out and thy coming in from this time forth, and even for evermore.

King James Version

THE LORD HIMSELF Watches OVER YOU

For Food,

WHERE MANY WALK IN HUNGER.

For Faith,

WHERE MANY WALK IN FEAR.

For Friends,

WHERE MANY WALK ALONE—

LORD,

WE ARE TRULY GRATEFUL.

Deuteronomy 8:7–10

7 For the Lord your God is bringing you into a good land, a land of brooks of water, of fountains and springs, flowing forth in valleys and hills;
8 a land of wheat and barley, of vines and fig trees and pomegranates, a land of olive oil and honey;
9 a land where you will eat food without scarcity, in which you will not lack anything; a land whose stones are iron, and out of whose hills you can dig copper.
10 When you have eaten and are satisfied, you shall bless the Lord your God for the good land which He has given you.

New American Standard Bible

Oh Lord my God!
When I in awesome wonder
Consider all the worlds
Thy hands have made,
I see the stars,
I hear the rolling thunder,
Thy power throughout
The universe displayed.

Then sings my soul,
My Savior, God, to Thee;
How great thou art,
How great thou art!

And when I think of God,
His son not sparing,
Sent Him to die,
I scarce can take it in;
That on the cross,
my burden
gladly bearing,
He bled and died
to take away my sin.

Carl Gustav Boberg

THEN
SINGS MY SOUL
MY SAVIOR
GOD TO THEE;
HOW GREAT THOU ART,
HOW GREAT
THOU ART!

TO WHAT WIL
LOOK for HEL
WILL NOT LOO
STRO
THAN YO

– C. S. LEWIS

t you

P IF YOU

K TO THAT

WHICH IS

NGER

URSELF?

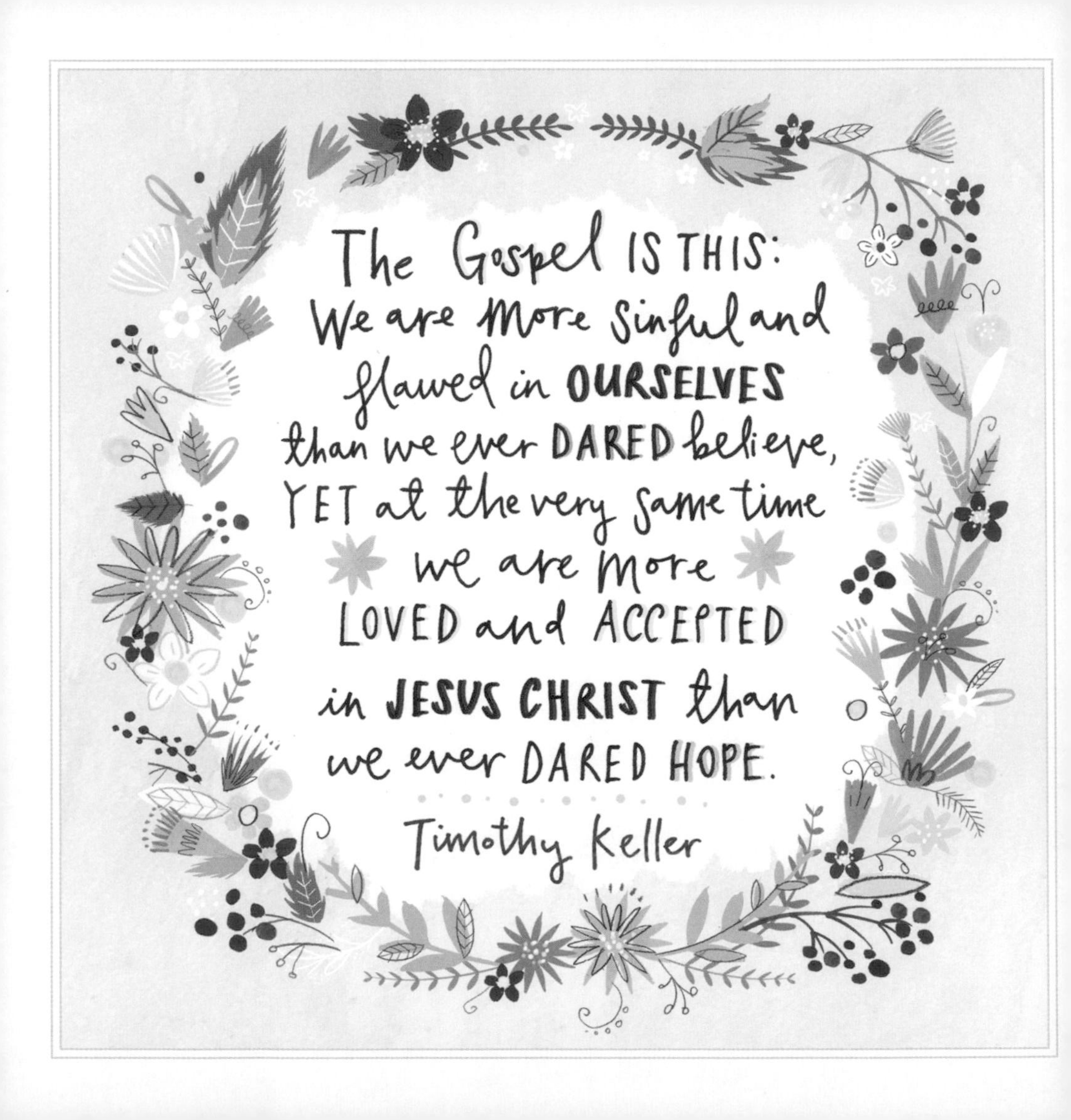
The Gospel IS THIS:
We are more sinful and
flawed in OURSELVES
than we ever DARED believe,
YET at the very same time
we are more
LOVED and ACCEPTED
in JESUS CHRIST than
we ever DARED HOPE.
Timothy Keller

2 Timothy 1:7–10

7 For God gave us not a spirit of fearfulness; but of power and love and discipline.
8 Be not ashamed therefore of the testimony of our Lord, nor of me his prisoner: but suffer hardship with the gospel according to the power of God;
9 who saved us, and called us with a holy calling, not according to our works, but according to his own purpose and grace, which was given us in Christ Jesus before times eternal,
10 but hath now been manifested by the appearing of our Saviour Christ Jesus, who abolished death, and brought life and immortality to light through the gospel,

American Standard Version

Mine eyes have seen the glory of the coming
of the Lord;
He is trampling out the vintage where the
grapes of wrath are stored;
He hath loosed the fateful lightning of His
terrible swift sword;
His truth is marching on.

Glory! Glory! Hallelujah!
Glory! Glory! Hallelujah!
Glory! Glory! Hallelujah!
His truth is marching on.

Julia W. Howe

Glory, Glory Hallelujah!

GOD IS
GOOD
ALL THE
TIME

Psalm 107:1–8

1 Give thanks to the Lord, for he is good!
His faithful love endures forever.
2 Has the Lord redeemed you? Then speak out!
Tell others he has redeemed you from your enemies.
3 For he has gathered the exiles from many lands,
from east and west,
from north and south.

4 Some wandered in the wilderness,
lost and homeless.
5 Hungry and thirsty,
they nearly died.
6 "Lord, help!" they cried in their trouble,
and he rescued them from their distress.
7 He led them straight to safety,
to a city where they could live.
8 Let them praise the Lord for his great love
and for the wonderful things he has done for them.

New Living Translation

God is Spirit,

and those who worship Him

must WORSHIP in

SPIRIT AND TRUTH

John 4:24 NASB

Ephesians 4:32

Be kind to one another, tender-hearted, forgiving each other, just as God in Christ also has forgiven you.

New American Standard Bible

FOR THE peace FROM above, FOR THE loving kindness OF God AND FOR THE salvation OF OUR souls, LET US pray TO THE Lord.

IT IS
WELL
WITH MY
SOUL.

When peace like a river, attendeth my way,
When sorrows like sea billows roll;
Whatever my lot,
Thou hast taught me to say
It is well, it is well, with my soul.

It is well, (it is well),
With my soul, (with my soul)
It is well, **it is well, with my soul.**

Though Satan should buffet, though trials should come,
Let this blest assurance control,
That Christ has regarded my helpless estate,
And hath shed His own blood for my soul.

Horatio Spafford

JOHN 15:9–13

9 Even as the Father has loved me, I also have loved you. Remain in my love.

10 If you keep my commandments, you will remain in my love; even as I have kept my Father's commandments, and remain in his love.

11 I have spoken these things to you, that my joy may remain in you, and that your joy may be made full.

12 "This is my commandment, that you love one another, even as I have loved you.

13 Greater love has no one than this, that someone lay down his life for his friends."

World English Bible

Love
LIKE
JESUS

Let thy goodness,
like a fetter,
BIND MY WANDERING
HEART to THEE.

PRONE to Wander, Lord,
I feel it,
PRONE to leave the God
I love.

Here's my heart,
O take and seal it,
Seal it for Thy
courts
above.
-Robert Robinson

THE ONLY ONE
who can
SATISFY
the human heart
IS THE ONE WHO
CREATED IT.

PSALM 136:1–9

1 Give thanks to the LORD, for he is good.
His love endures forever.

2 Give thanks to the God of gods.
His love endures forever.

3 Give thanks to the Lord of lords:
His love endures forever.

4 to him who alone does great wonders,
His love endures forever.

5 who by his understanding made the heavens,
His love endures forever.

6 who spread out the earth upon the waters,
His love endures forever.

7 who made the great lights—
His love endures forever.

8 the sun to govern the day,
His love endures forever.

9 the moon and stars to govern the night;
His love endures forever.

New International Version

Hebrews 13:5b–9a

5b For God has said,

"I will never fail you.
I will never abandon you."

6 So we can say with confidence,
"The Lord is my helper,
so I will have no fear.
What can mere people do to me?"

7 Remember your leaders who taught you the word of God. Think of all the good that has come from their lives, and follow the example of their faith.

8 Jesus Christ is the same yesterday, today, and forever.

9a So do not be attracted by strange, new ideas. Your strength comes from God's grace.

New Living Translation

LET YOUR
FAITH
BE
BIGGER
THAN
YOUR
FEAR

Lord
Make Me an
instrument
of your peace

Lord, make me an instrument of Your peace.
Where there is hatred, let me sow love; where there is injury, pardon; where there is doubt, faith; where there is despair, hope; where there is darkness, light; where there is sadness, joy.

Grant that I may not so much seek to be consoled as to console; to be understood as to understand; to be loved as to love; For it is in giving that we receive; it is in pardoning that we are pardoned; it is in dying that we are born again to eternal life.

The Prayer of St. Francis

MAY GOD
HOLD

YOU
IN THE PALM
OF
HIS HAND.

Job 36:26–32

26 Surely God is great, and we do not know him;
the number of his years is unsearchable.
27 For he draws up the drops of water;
he distills his mist in rain,
28 which the skies pour down
and drop upon mortals abundantly.
29 Can anyone understand the spreading of the clouds,
the thunderings of his pavilion?
30 See, he scatters his lightning around him
and covers the roots of the sea.
31 For by these he governs peoples;
he gives food in abundance.
32 He covers his hands with the lightning,
and commands it to strike the mark.

New Revised Standard Version

Consider what you owe
to His immutability.
Though you have changed
a thousand times,
He has not changed once.
Charles Spurgeon

HERE I AM.

Send me!

Isaiah 6:8

I heard the Lord's voice, saying, "Whom shall I send, and who will go for us?"

Then I said, **"Here I am. Send me!"**

World English Bible

I believe in God, the Father Almighty,
maker of heaven and earth;
I believe in Jesus Christ his only Son, our Lord;
who was conceived by the Holy Spirit, born of the Virgin
Mary, suffered under Pontius Pilate, was crucified, dead,
and buried;
on the third day he rose again from the dead;
he ascended into heaven, and sitteth at the right hand
of God the Father Almighty;
from thence he shall come to judge the quick and the dead.
I believe in the Holy Spirit, the holy catholic church,
the communion of saints, the forgiveness of sins,
the resurrection of the body, and the life everlasting.
Amen.

The Apostle's Creed

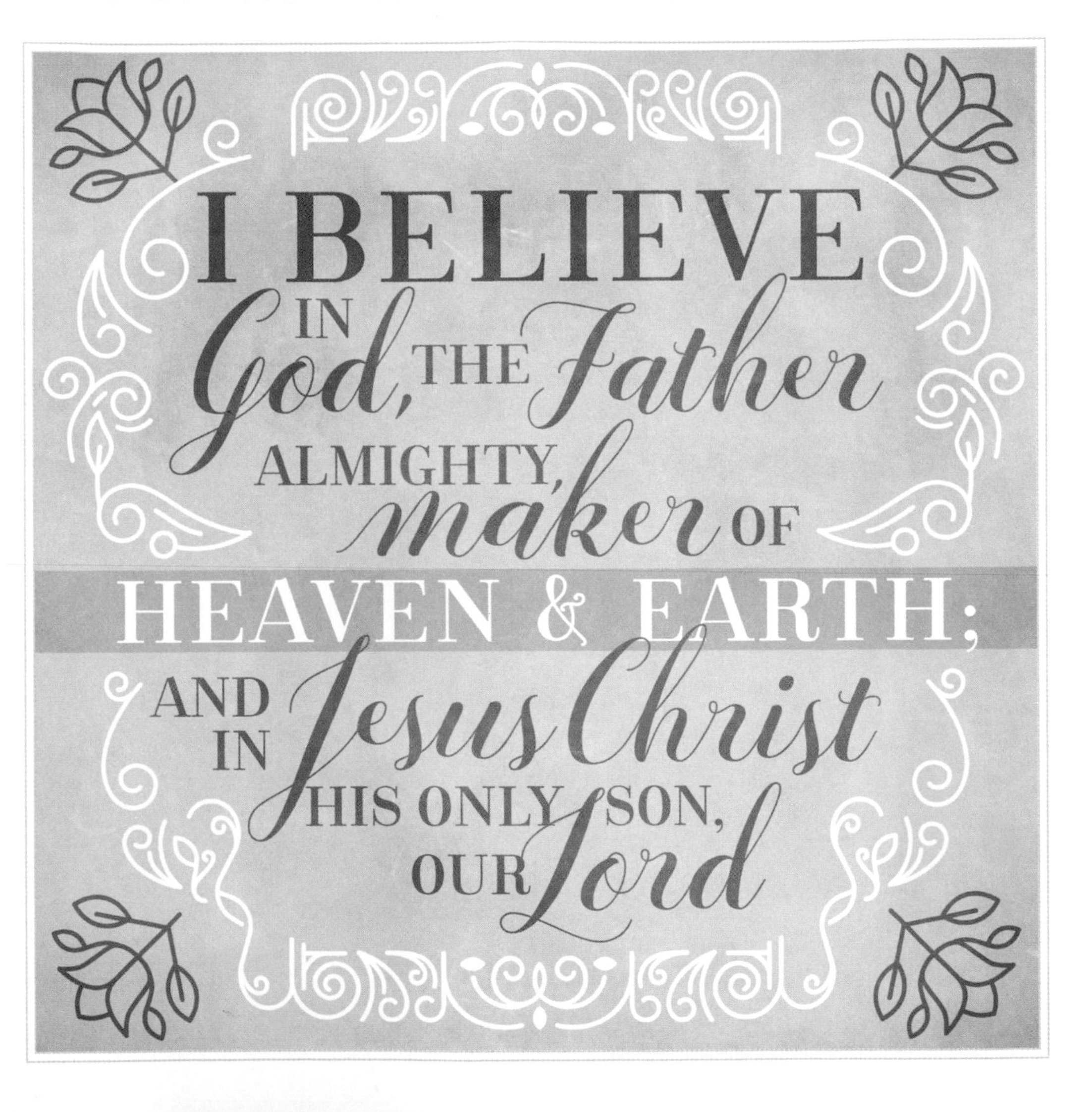
I BELIEVE
IN God, THE Father
ALMIGHTY, maker OF
HEAVEN & EARTH;
AND IN Jesus Christ
HIS ONLY SON,
OUR Lord

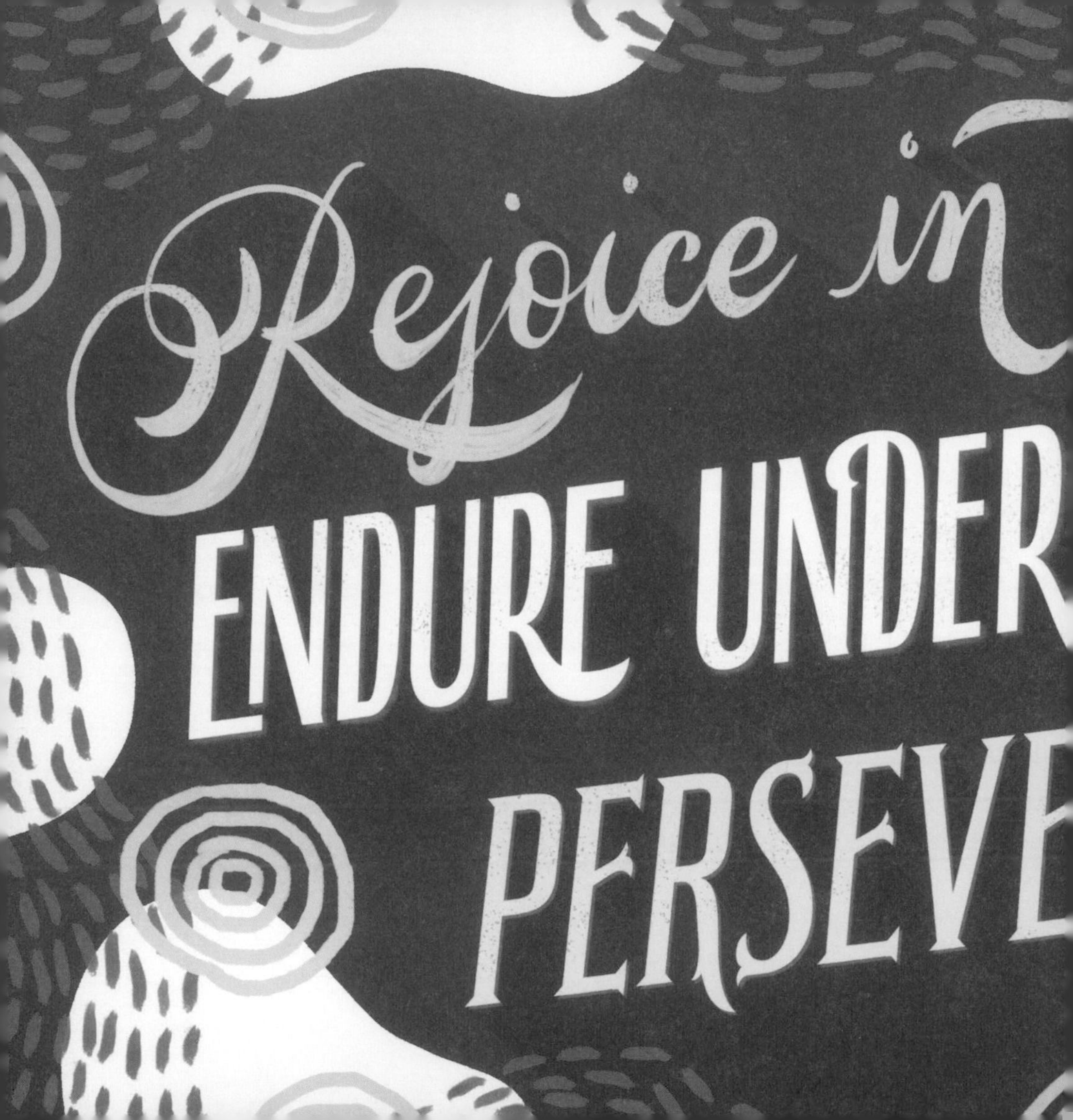
Rejoice in
ENDURE UNDER
PERSEVE

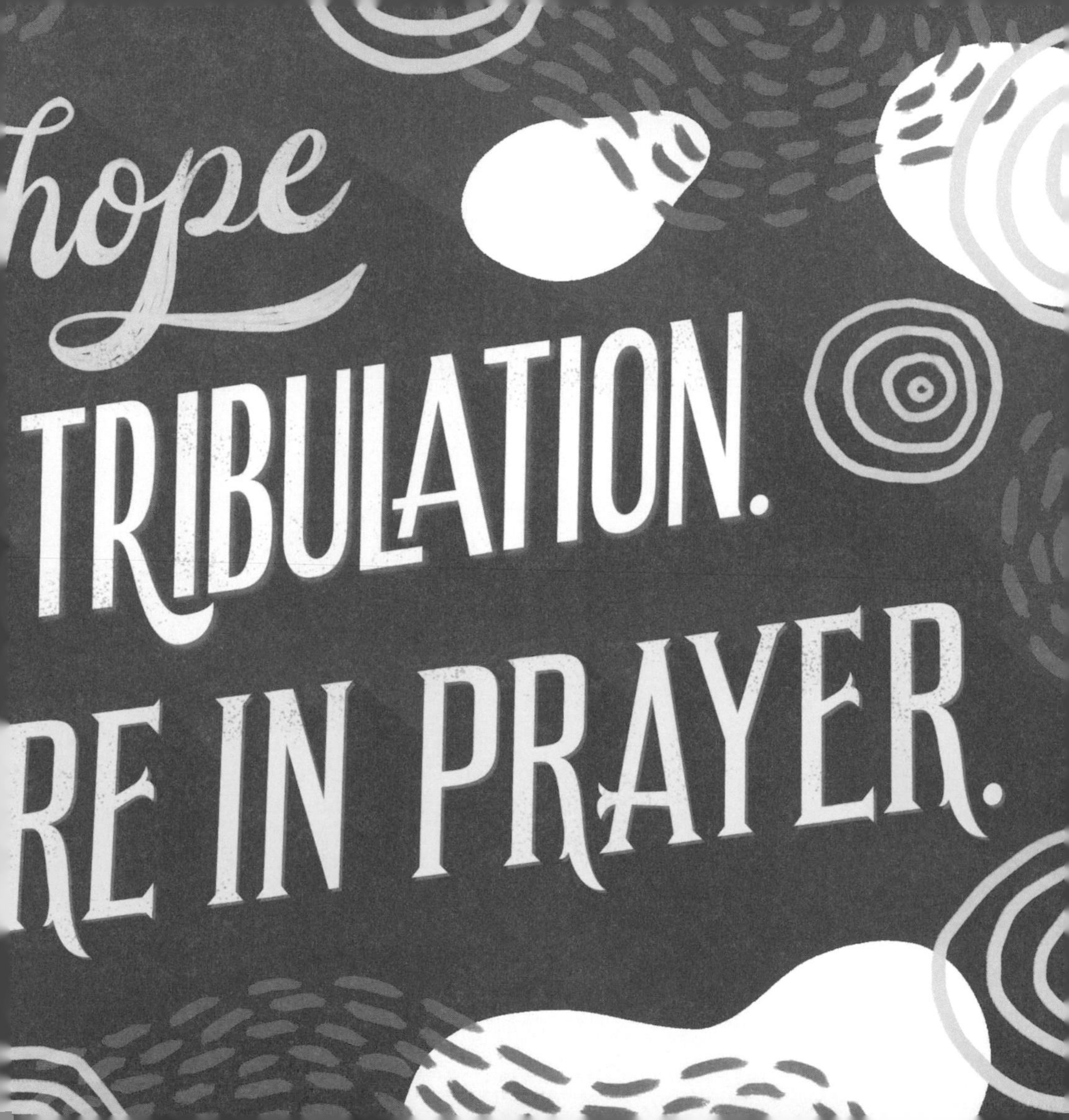
hope
TRIBULATION.
RE IN PRAYER.

PRAYER
is a door into
the HOSPITALITY of
GOD'S HOME

Psalm 34:4–7

4 I prayed to the Lord, and he answered me.
He freed me from all my fears.

5 Those who look to him for help will be radiant with joy;
no shadow of shame will darken their faces.

6 In my desperation I prayed, and the Lord listened;
he saved me from all my troubles.

7 For the angel of the Lord is a guard;
he surrounds and defends all who fear him.

New Living Translation

LUKE 6:35–36

35 But love your enemies, and do good, and lend, expecting nothing in return; and your reward will be great, and you will be sons of the Most High; for He Himself is kind to ungrateful and evil men. **36** Be merciful, just as your Father is merciful.

New American Standard Bible

DO SMALL THINGS WITH GREAT LOVE

WHAT IS SEEN is
TEMPORARY:
WHAT IS UNSEEN
is ETERNAL.

2 Corinthians 4:16–18

16 So we do not lose heart. Even though our outer nature is wasting away, our inner nature is being renewed day by day.

17 For this slight momentary affliction is preparing us for an eternal weight of glory beyond all measure,

18 because we look not at what can be seen but at what cannot be seen; for what can be seen is temporary, but what cannot be seen is eternal.

New Revised Standard Version

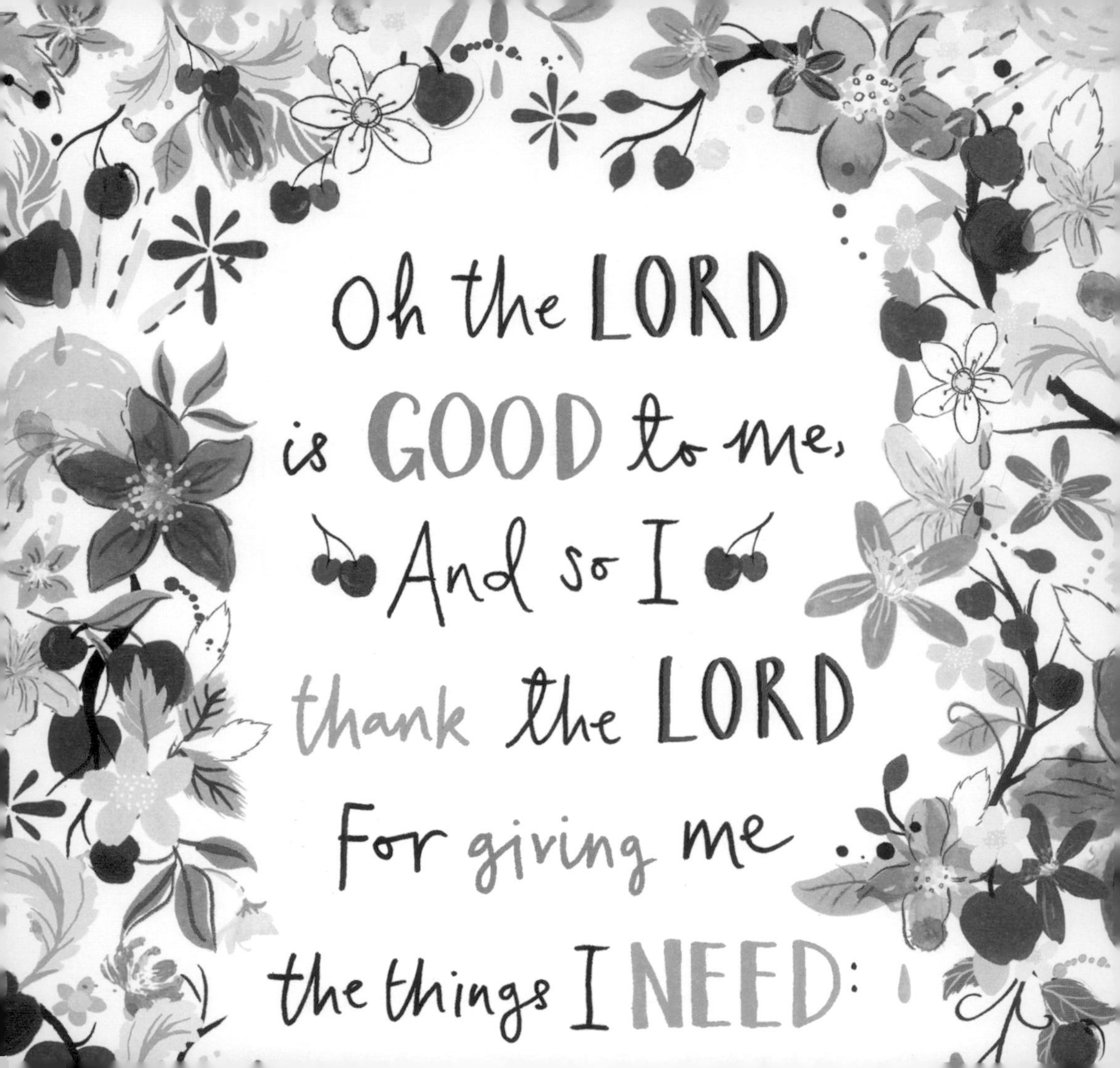
Oh the LORD
is GOOD to me,
And so I
thank the LORD
For giving me
the things I NEED:

The SUN,
and the RAIN,
and the
APPLE SEED;
The LORD is
GOOD to me.

PHILIPPIANS 4:4–7

4 **Rejoice in the Lord always.** Again I will say, rejoice!

5 Let your gentleness be known to all men. The Lord is at hand.

6 Be anxious for nothing, but in everything by prayer and supplication, with thanksgiving, let your requests be made known to God;
7 and the peace of God, which surpasses all understanding, will guard your hearts and minds through Christ Jesus.

New King James Version

Rejoice in the LORD ALWAYS

ALMIGHTY GOD,
TO YOU
ALL HEARTS ARE OPEN,
ALL DESIRES KNOWN,
& FROM YOU
NO SECRETS
ARE HID

Almighty God, to you all hearts are open, all desires known, and from you no secrets are hid: Cleanse the thoughts of our hearts by the inspiration of your Holy Spirit, that we may perfectly love you, and worthily magnify your holy Name; through Christ our Lord. Amen.

The Book of Common Prayer

Romans 5:18–21

18 Yes, Adam's one sin brings condemnation for everyone, but Christ's one act of righteousness brings a right relationship with God and new life for everyone.
19 Because one person disobeyed God, many became sinners. But because one other person obeyed God, many will be made righteous.

20 God's law was given so that all people could see how sinful they were. But as people sinned more and more, God's wonderful grace became more abundant.
21 So just as sin ruled over all people and brought them to death, now God's wonderful grace rules instead, giving us right standing with God and resulting in eternal life through Jesus Christ our Lord.

New LIving Translation

Grace
CHANGES
Everything

GOD grant ME
the SERENITY
to ACCEPT
THE THINGS i CANNOT
CHANGE,
COURAGE

to CHANGE the
THINGS i can,
(&)
WISDOM to KNOW
the DIFFERENCE.

REINHOLD NIEBUHR

you are
fearfully
and
Wonderfully
made

Psalm 139:11–14

11 If I say, "Surely the darkness will overwhelm me;
the light around me will be night";
12 even the darkness doesn't hide from you,
but the night shines as the day.
The darkness is like light to you.
13 For you formed my inmost being.
You knit me together in my mother's womb.
14 I will give thanks to you,
for I am fearfully and wonderfully made.
Your works are wonderful.
My soul knows that very well.

World English Bible

Proverbs 3:1–4

1 My son, do not forget my teaching,
But let your heart keep my commandments;
2 For length of days and years of life
And peace they will add to you.
3 Do not let kindness and truth leave you;
Bind them around your neck,
Write them on the tablet of your heart.
4 So you will find favor and good repute
In the sight of God and man.

New American Standard Bible

you can save
HEARTS
&
LIVES
with Grace
-Jen Hatmaker

GIVE US THIS DAY

Our

DAILY

bread

Matthew 6:9–13

9 After this manner, therefore pray ye: Our Father which art in heaven, Hallowed be thy name.
10 Thy kingdom come, Thy will be done in earth, as it is in heaven.
11 Give us this day our daily bread.
12 And forgive us our debts, as we forgive our debtors.
13 And lead us not into temptation, but deliver us from evil: For thine is the kingdom, and the power, and the glory, for ever. Amen.

King James Version

BRING ME
TO A CLEARER
KNOWING OF
THE

MYSTERY

FIRST Bore ME

FROM

DARK

J. Philip Newell

Psalm 119:133–136

133 Establish my footsteps in your word.
Don't let any iniquity have dominion over me.
134 Redeem me from the oppression of man,
so I will observe your precepts.
135 Make your face shine on your servant.
Teach me your statutes.
136 Streams of tears run down my eyes,
because they don't observe your law.

World English Bible

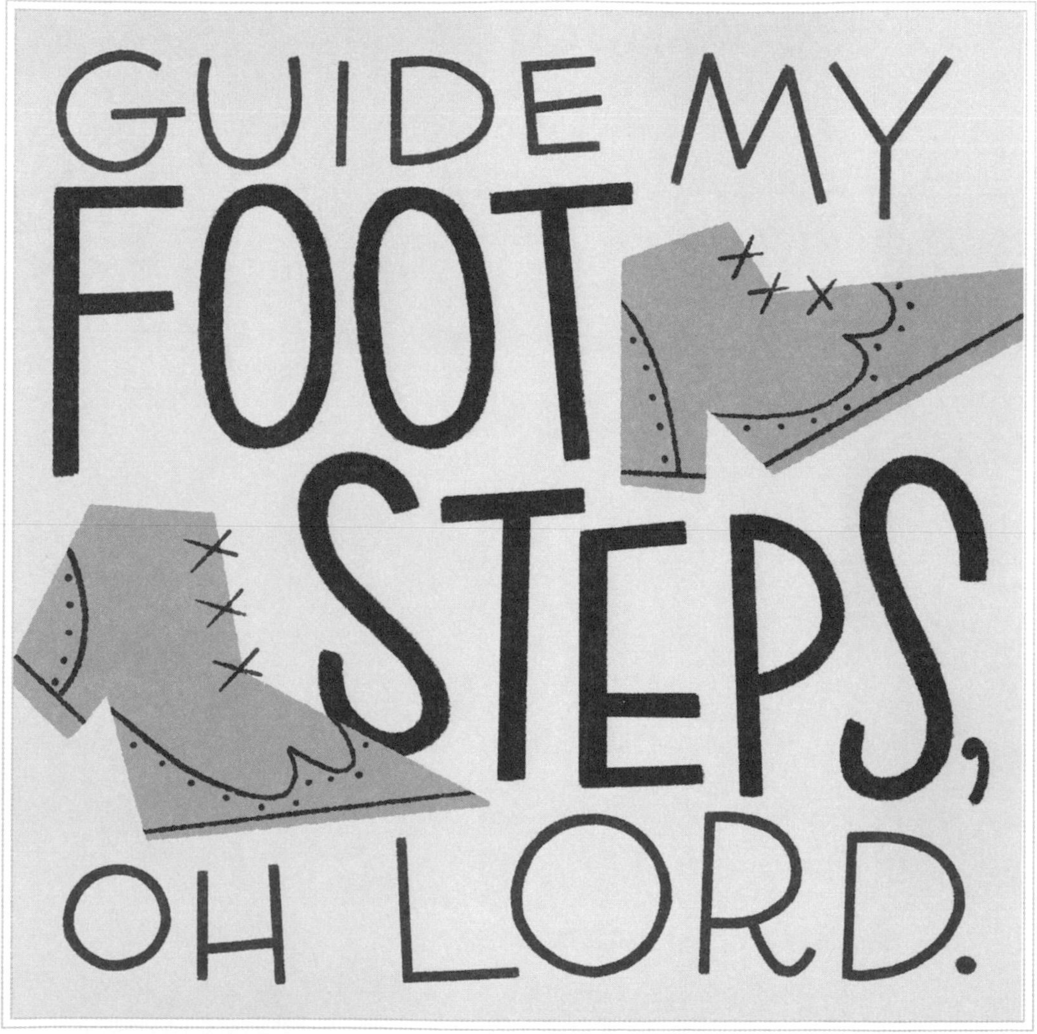

GUIDE MY FOOTSTEPS, OH LORD.

When I survey the
wondrous cross,
on which the
Prince of glory died,
my richest gain
I count but loss,
and pour contempt
on all my pride.

When I survey the wondrous cross,
On which the Prince of glory died,
My richest gain I count but loss,
And pour contempt on all my pride.

Forbid it, Lord, that I should boast,
Save in the death of Christ, my God:
All the vain things that charm me most,
I sacrifice them to His blood.

See, from His head, His hands, His feet,
Sorrow and love flow mingled down:
Did e'er such love and sorrow meet,
Or thorns compose so rich a crown?

Were the whole realm of nature mine,
That were a present far too small:
Love so amazing, so divine,
Demands my soul, my life, my all.

Isaac Watts

MATTHEW 6:25–26

25 Therefore I tell you, don't be anxious for your life: what you will eat, or what you will drink; nor yet for your body, what you will wear. Isn't life more than food, and the body more than clothing?
26 See the birds of the sky, that they don't sow, neither do they reap, nor gather into barns. Your heavenly Father feeds them. Aren't you of much more value than they?

World English Bible

PRAY
more
WORRY
LESS

MAN IS BORN BROKEN.
HE LIVES BY
MENDING.

THE
GRACE OF GOD
IS
GLUE!
EUGENE O' NEILL

INHALE
Faith
exhale
FEAR

ISAIAH 41:8–10

8 "But you, Israel, my servant,
Jacob, whom I have chosen,
you descendants of Abraham my friend,
9 I took you from the ends of the earth,
from its farthest corners I called you.
I said, 'You are my servant';
I have chosen you and have not rejected you.
10 So do not fear, for I am with you;
do not be dismayed, for I am your God.
I will strengthen you and help you;
I will uphold you with my righteous right hand."

New International Version

John 1: 6–13

6 There was a man sent from God whose name was John.
7 He came as a witness to testify concerning
that light, so that through him all might believe.
8 He himself was not the light; he came only as a witness
to the light.

9 The true light that gives light to everyone was coming
into the world.
10 He was in the world, and though the world was made
through him, the world did not recognize him.
11 He came to that which was his own, but his own did
not receive him.
12 Yet to all who did receive him, to those who believed in
his name, he gave the right to become children of God—
13 children born not of natural descent, nor of human
decision or a husband's will, but born of God.

New international Version

CHRIST
is not ONLY our way
HE IS THE
LIGHT UPON THE WAY...
Nothing BUT LIGHT
WILL DISPEL
THE DARKNESS
—D.L. MOODY

god

IS ALWAYS UP TO

something

Lamentations 3:22–26

22 The steadfast love of the Lord never ceases,
his mercies never come to an end;
23 they are new every morning;
great is your faithfulness.
24 "The Lord is my portion," says my soul,
"therefore I will hope in him."

25 The Lord is good to those who wait for him,
to the soul that seeks him.
26 It is good that one should wait quietly for the
salvation of the Lord.

New Revised Standard Version

ALL THINGS
BRIGHT
&
BEAUTIFUL,
ALL CREATURES
GREAT
&
SMALL

ALL THINGS
WISE
&
WONDERFUL,
THE LORD GOD
MADE THEM
ALL
- Cecil Alexander

Hebrews 6:13–20

13 For when God made a promise to Abraham, since he could swear by no one greater, he swore by himself,
14 saying, "Surely blessing I will bless you, and multiplying I will multiply you."
15 Thus, having patiently endured, he obtained the promise.
16 For men indeed swear by a greater one, and in every dispute of theirs the oath is final for confirmation.
17 In this way God, being determined to show more abundantly to the heirs of the promise the immutability of his counsel, interposed with an oath;
18 that by two immutable things, in which it is impossible for God to lie, we may have a strong encouragement, who have fled for refuge to take hold of the hope set before us.
19 This hope we have as an anchor of the soul, a hope both sure and steadfast and entering into that which is within the veil;
20 where as a forerunner Jesus entered for us, having become a high priest forever after the order of Melchizedek.

World English Bible

WE HAVE THIS
HOPE
AS AN
ANCHOR
FOR
THE SOUL

PRAISE HIM ABOVE,
ye heavenly host;
PRAISE
FATHER, SON,
AND
HOLY GHOST.

Awake, my soul, and with the sun
Thy daily stage of duty run;
Shake off dull sloth, and early rise,
To pay thy morning sacrifice.

Praise God, from Whom all blessings flow;
Praise Him, all creatures here below;
Praise Him above, ye heavenly host;
Praise Father, Son, and Holy Ghost.

Thomas Ken

Philippians 2:13–18

13 For it is God who works in you both to will and to work, for his good pleasure.

14 Do all things without murmurings and disputes,

15 that you may become blameless and harmless, children of God without defect in the middle of a crooked and perverse generation, among whom you are seen as lights in the world,

16 holding up the word of life; that I may have something to boast in the day of Christ, that I didn't run in vain nor labor in vain.

17 Yes, and if I am poured out on the sacrifice and service of your faith, I rejoice, and rejoice with you all.

18 In the same way, you also rejoice, and rejoice with me.

World English Bible

DON'T LET ME EVER THINK,
dear God,
THAT I WAS ANYTHING
BUT THE INSTRUMENT
FOR
Your story...

Flannery O'Connor

GOD IS W
ALW

TH YOU
AYS

JESUS SAID,

You Do Not Know

WHAT I AM DOING, BUT LATER

You Will Understand

John 13:3–10a

3 Jesus, knowing that the Father had given all things into his hands, and that he came from God, and was going to God,
4 arose from supper, and laid aside his outer garments. He took a towel, and wrapped a towel around his waist.
5 Then he poured water into the basin, and began to wash the disciples' feet, and to wipe them with the towel that was wrapped around him.
6 Then he came to Simon Peter. He said to him, "Lord, do you wash my feet?"

7 Jesus answered him, "You don't know what I am doing now, but you will understand later."

8 Peter said to him, "You will never wash my feet!"

Jesus answered him, "If I don't wash you, you have no part with me."

9 Simon Peter said to him, "Lord, not my feet only, but also my hands and my head!"

10 Jesus said to him, "Someone who has bathed only needs to have his feet washed, but is completely clean."

World English Bible

MICAH 7:18–20

18 Where is another God like you,
who pardons the guilt of the remnant,
overlooking the sins of his special people?
You will not stay angry with your people forever,
because you delight in showing unfailing love.
19 Once again you will have compassion on us.
You will trample our sins under your feet
and throw them into the depths of the ocean!
20 You will show us your faithfulness and unfailing love
as you promised to our ancestors Abraham and Jacob long ago.

New Living Translation

Delight to Show Mercy

WHEN LIFE GETS TOO HARD TO STAND, KNEEL.

Hebrews 4:14–16

14 Therefore since we have a great high priest who has passed through the heavens, Jesus, the Son of God, let us hold fast our confession.

15 For we do not have a high priest who cannot sympathize with our weaknesses, but One who has been tempted in all things as *we are, yet* without sin.

16 Therefore, let us draw near with confidence to the throne of grace, so that we may receive mercy and find grace to help in time of need.

New American Standard Bible

EVERY DAY
SOME NEW

E MAY SEE
NG IN CHRIST
SAMUEL RUTHERFORD

Philippians 4:11b–13

11b I have learned to be content in whatever circumstances I am.
12 I know how to get along with humble means, and I also know how to live in prosperity; in any and every circumstance I have learned the secret of being filled and going hungry, both of having abundance and suffering need.
13 I can do all things through Him who strengthens me.

New American Standard Bible

Count
YOUR
Blessings

HE MUST BECOME

GREATER

I MUST BECOME

Less

John 3:29–36

29 He who has the bride is the bridegroom; but the friend of the bridegroom, who stands and hears him, rejoices greatly because of the bridegroom's voice. This, my joy, therefore is made full.

30 He must increase, but I must decrease.

31 He who comes from above is above all. He who is from the earth belongs to the earth, and speaks of the earth. He who comes from heaven is above all.

32 What he has seen and heard, of that he testifies; and no one receives his witness.

33 He who has received his witness has set his seal to this, that God is true.

34 For he whom God has sent speaks the words of God; for God gives the Spirit without measure.

35 The Father loves the Son, and has given all things into his hand.

36 One who believes in the Son has eternal life, but one who disobeys the Son won't see life, but the wrath of God remains on him.

World English Bible

1 JOHN 4:13–16

13 Hereby know we that we dwell in him, and he in us, because he hath given us of his Spirit.

14 And we have seen and do testify that the Father sent the Son to be the Saviour of the world.

15 Whosoever shall confess that Jesus is the Son of God, God dwelleth in him, and he in God.

16 And we have known and believed the love that God hath to us. God is love; and he that dwelleth in love dwelleth in God, and God in him.

King James Version

CHRIST OUR
Passover
IS SACRIFICED FOR
US.

the love you GIVE & RECEIVE is a reality that will Lead You CLOSER & CLOSER TO GOD as well as to those whom God has given you

TO LOVE

-Henri J. M. Nouwen-

GOD has a Plan

JEREMIAH 29:11–14

11 For I know the plans I have for you," declares the LORD, "plans to prosper you and not to harm you, plans to give you hope and a future.
12 Then you will call on me and come and pray to me, and I will listen to you.
13 You will seek me and find me when you seek me with all your heart.
14 I will be found by you," declares the LORD, "and will bring you back from captivity. I will gather you from all the nations and places where I have banished you," declares the LORD, "and will bring you back to the place from which I carried you into exile."

New International Version

JAMES 1:17–18

17 Every good gift and every perfect gift is from above, coming down from the Father of lights, with whom can be no variation, nor turning shadow.
18 Of his own will he gave birth to us by the word of truth, that we should be a kind of first fruits of his creatures.

World English Bible

Bless the food before us,
the family beside us,
& the Love Between us

Go, tell it on the mountain,
over the hills
and everywhere;
go, tell it on the
mountain,
that Jesus Christ
is born.

Go, tell it on the mountain,
Over the hills and everywhere;
Go, tell it on the mountain
That Jesus Christ is born.

While shepherds kept their watching
Over silent flocks by night,
Behold, throughout the heavens
There shone a holy light.

Go, tell it on the mountain,
Over the hills and everywhere;
Go, tell it on the mountain
That Jesus Christ is born.

Down in a lowly manger
Our humble Christ was born,
And God sent us salvation
That blessed Christmas morn.

Go, tell it on the mountain,
Over the hills and everywhere;
Go, tell it on the mountain
That Jesus Christ is born.

John Wesley Work Jr.

It is right, and a
good and joyful thing,
always and everywhere
to give thanks to you,
Father Almighty, Creator
of heaven & earth.

Zephaniah 3:15–17

15 The Lord has taken away *His* judgments against you,

He has cleared away your enemies.

The King of Israel, the Lord, is in your midst;

You will fear disaster no more.

16 In that day it will be said to Jerusalem:

"Do not be afraid, O Zion;

Do not let your hands fall limp.

17 "The Lord your God is in your midst,

A victorious warrior.

He will exult over you with joy,

He will be quiet in His love,

He will rejoice over you with shouts of joy."

New American Standard Bible

He is MIGHTY to SAVE

WE MUST BE READY
to
ALLOW OURSELVES TO BE
INTERRUPTED
by
God.
DIETRICH BONHOEFFER

PSALM 46:1–3, 7

1 God is our refuge and strength,

A very present help in trouble.

2 Therefore we will not fear, though the earth should change

And though the mountains slip into the heart of the sea;

3 Though its waters roar *and* foam,

Though the mountains quake at its swelling pride.

7 The LORD of hosts is with us;

The God of Jacob is our stronghold.

New American Standard Bible

1 Corinthians 13:8–13

8 Love never fails. But where there are prophecies, they will be done away with. Where there are various languages, they will cease. Where there is knowledge, it will be done away with.
9 For we know in part, and we prophesy in part;
10 but when that which is complete has come, then that which is partial will be done away with.
11 When I was a child, I spoke as a child, I felt as a child, I thought as a child. Now that I have become a man, I have put away childish things.
12 For now we see in a mirror, dimly, but then face to face. Now I know in part, but then I will know fully, even as I was also fully known.
13 But now faith, hope, and love remain—these three. The greatest of these is love.

World English Bible

Faith
HOPE
Love

All ye who are
of tender heart,
forgiving others
take your part.

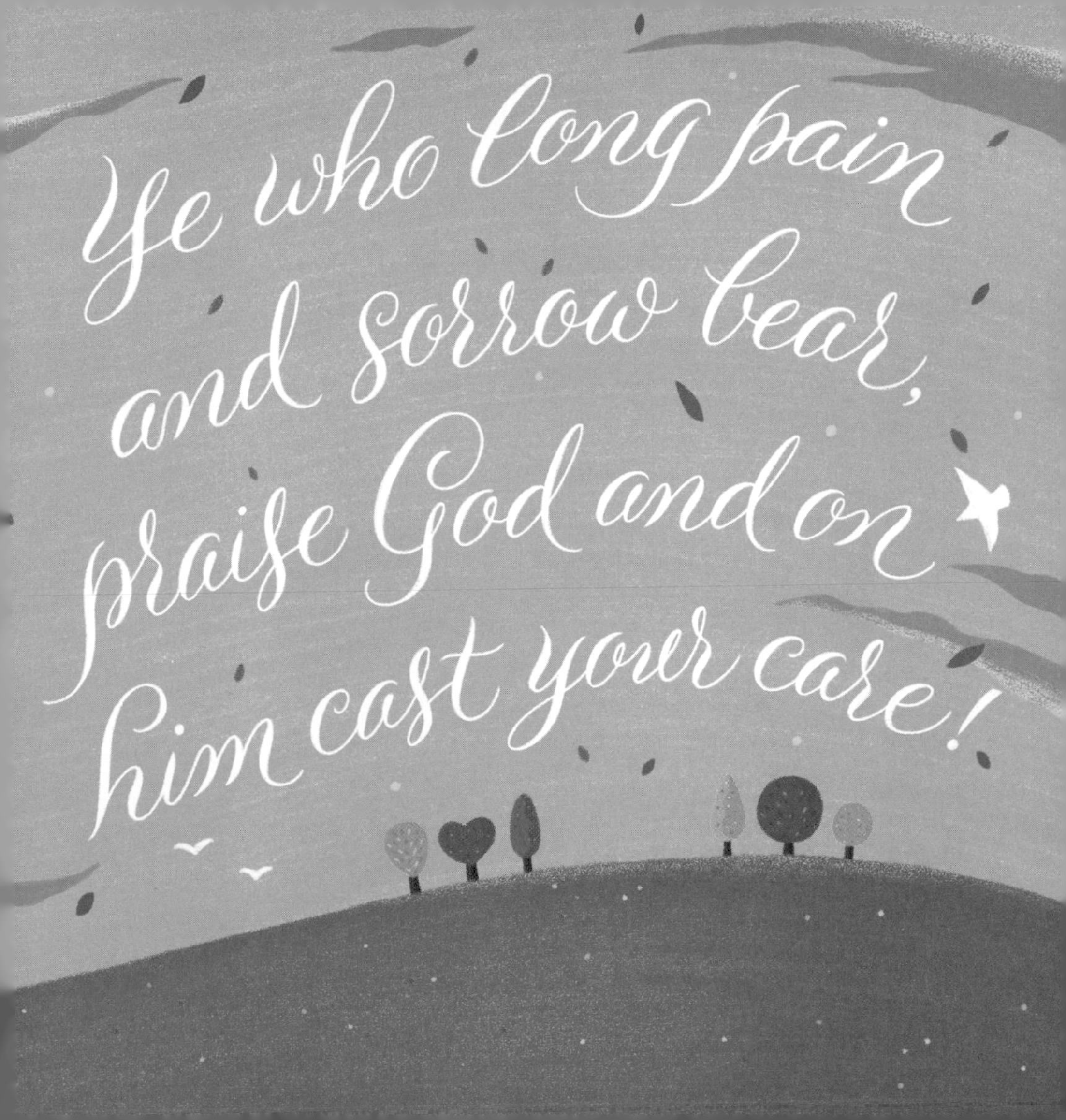

Ye who long pain
and sorrow bear,
praise God and on
him cast your care!

2 PETER 1:3–4

3 By his divine power, God has given us everything we need for a godly life. We have received all of this by coming to know him, the one who called us to himself by means of his marvelous glory and excellence.
4 And because of his glory and excellence, he has given us great and precious promises. These are the promises that enable you to share his divine nature and escape the world's corruption caused by human desires.

New Living Translation

WE ARE SO

BLESSED

The World is Charged with the Grandeur ... of ... GOD

~Gerard Manley Hopkins

Job 37:10–16

10 By the breath of God ice is given,
And the broad waters are frozen.
11 Also with moisture He saturates the thick clouds;
He scatters His bright clouds.
12 And they swirl about, being turned by His guidance,
That they may do whatever He commands them
On the face of the whole earth.
13 He causes it to come,
Whether for correction,
Or for His land,
Or for mercy.

14 "Listen to this, O Job;
Stand still and consider the wondrous works of God.
15 Do you know when God dispatches them,
And causes the light of His cloud to shine?
16 Do you know how the clouds are balanced,
Those wondrous works of Him who is perfect in knowledge?"

New King James Version

O for a thousand tongues to sing
my great Redeemer's praise,
the glories of my God and King,
the triumphs of his grace!

My gracious Master and my God,
assist me to proclaim,
to spread thro' all the earth abroad
the honors of your name.

Jesus! the name that charms our fears,
that bids our sorrows cease,
'tis music in the sinner's ears,
'tis life and health and peace.

He breaks the power of cancelled sin,
he sets the prisoner free;
his blood can make the foulest clean;
his blood availed for me.

To God all glory, praise, and love
be now and ever given
by saints below and saints above,
the Church in earth and heaven.

Charles Wesley

O for a thousand tongues
to sing
My great Redeemer's praise,
The glories of my God and King,
The triumphs of
His Grace!

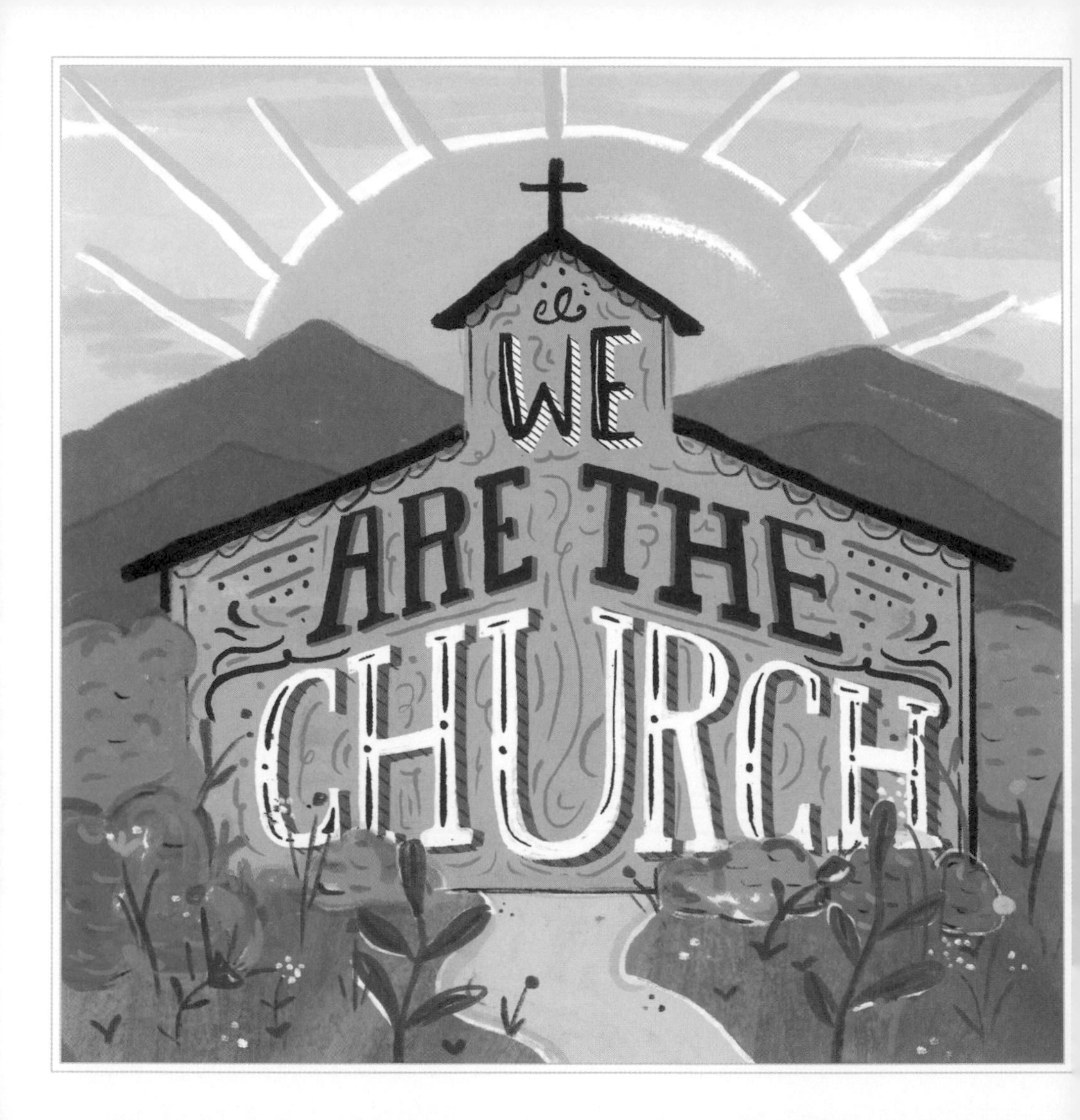
WE
ARE THE
CHURCH

Ephesians 4:11–16

11 So Christ himself gave the apostles, the prophets, the evangelists, the pastors and teachers,
12 to equip his people for works of service, so that the body of Christ may be built up
13 until we all reach unity in the faith and in the knowledge of the Son of God and become mature, attaining to the whole measure of the fullness of Christ.

14 Then we will no longer be infants, tossed back and forth by the waves, and blown here and there by every wind of teaching and by the cunning and craftiness of people in their deceitful scheming.
15 Instead, speaking the truth in love, we will grow to become in every respect the mature body of him who is the head, that is, Christ.
16 From him the whole body, joined and held together by every supporting ligament, grows and builds itself up in love, as each part does its work.

New International Version

THIS IS MY STORY, MY SA

PRAISING MY SA

all the

THIS
is
my
SONG,
IOR
day long.

Revelation 5:11–13

11 I saw, and I heard something like a voice of many angels around the throne, the living creatures, and the elders; and the number of them was ten thousands of ten thousands, and thousands of thousands;
12 saying with a loud voice, "Worthy is the Lamb who has been killed to receive the power, wealth, wisdom, strength, honor, glory, and blessing!"

13 I heard every created thing which is in heaven, on the earth, under the earth, on the sea, and everything in them, saying, "To him who sits on the throne, and to the Lamb be the blessing, the honor, the glory, and the dominion, forever and ever! Amen!"

World English Bible

Worthy is
the Lamb
who was
Slain

Let go and Let God

JAMES 1:2–6

2 My brothers and sisters, whenever you face trials of any kind, consider it nothing but joy,
3 because you know that the testing of your faith produces endurance;
4 and let endurance have its full effect, so that you may be mature and complete, lacking in nothing.

5 If any of you is lacking in wisdom, ask God, who gives to all generously and ungrudgingly, and it will be given you.
6 But ask in faith, never doubting, for the one who doubts is like a wave of the sea, driven and tossed by the wind.

New Revised Standard Version

I do not
AT ALL
understand
THE MYSTERY
of grace –

ONLY THAT
IT MEETS US
where we are
BUT DOES NOT
LEAVE US
where it found us.

—ANNE LAMOTT

1 Chronicles 16:35–36

35 Say also:

"Save us, O God of our salvation,
    and gather and rescue us from among the nations,
that we may give thanks to your holy name,
    and glory in your praise.
36 Blessed be the Lord, the God of Israel,
    from everlasting to everlasting."

Then all the people said "Amen!" and praised the Lord.

New Revised Standard Version

AND ALL THE
PEOPLE
SAID
AMEN

About the Artists

Being an illustrator lights **Kelly Angelovic** up. It makes her soul sparkle. Specializing in hand lettering, illustration, and surface pattern design, she also loves to play with packaging, editorial design, and children's picture books. A Colorado native, she resides with her family in Boulder. When she's not working in her studio, she can often be found playing outside with her family. **(pages 64–65, 115, 119, 157)**

Jaclyn Atkinson is an artist and illustrator from the Blue Ridge Mountains residing in her chosen home of Brooklyn. Her illustrations begin as woodcut relief prints before adding digital color. When not carving or reading, she is dreaming up ways to engage others through art and performance. **(pages 30, 61, 88–89, 147)**

Caitlin Bristow is a wife, mom, and the hand-letterer behind Lettered Life. She loves being an illustrator with words and her fluid, upbeat lettering style includes a little flourish, bringing a fresh feel to all that she creates. She's blessed to the brim and lives outside Charlotte, North Carolina. **(pages 23, 62, 122, 168–169)**

Becca Cahan is a Boston-based MassArt graduate who focuses on watercolor hand-lettered illustrations. She thrives on creating happy and colorful pieces of art with lots of curvature and geometric patterning. Becca loves creating art for tactile gift products that people can use every day. **(pages 26, 106, 120–121, 203)**

Veronica Chen is an illustrator based in New York. From illustrated lettering to surface design and everything in between, her work has been recognized and featured in *3x3* magazine and *American Illustration*. When she isn't drawing for clients, she keeps herself busy with personal and DIY projects, some of which can be found in her Etsy shop. **(pages 20, 80–81, 167, 180)**

Cyla Costa is a lettering artist, illustrator and daydreamer—not necessarily in that order. She studied graphic design in Brazil, specialized in illustration in Barcelona, and studied typeface design in NYC. She works with lettering, branding, illustration, printing, and painting: mainly with all things related to letters. Her one-woman studio is (mostly) in Curitiba, Brazil. Visit cylacosta.com / follow @cylacosta **(pages 78, 135, 160–161, 198)**

Mye De Leon is a lettering artist and illustrator based in Singapore. The engineering graduate pursued her love for letterforms after publishing her first coloring book with Mini-Lou called *The Little Alphabet Book of Hand-Lettered Type*. She has since worked for a wide range of clients globally while in pursuit of sharing her talent with others who want to learn the beauty of writing letters. **(pages 3, 13, 32–33, 46)**

Inspired by her faith and influenced by her love of color and trends, Stephanie Sliwinski enjoys creating art prints to encourage and brighten your day. She's the artist behind **Fancy That Design House & Co.**, and when she's not designing, she's chasing around her three boys and backyard chickens. You can find Stephanie at fancythatdesignhouse.com and on Instagram @fancythatdesignhouse. **(pages 48–49, 55, 103, 151)**

Vaughn Fender is an artist residing in the Northeast. Born in Kingston, Jamaica, he is inspired by vibrant colors, bustling streets, and music with good vibes.

Working primarily in the areas of design and illustration, he divides his time between drawing, hand-drawn letters, humor, booming colors, and lots of notemaking. **(pages 39, 72–73, 93, 164)**

Holly Graham is an illustrator based in Brooklyn. She specializes in colorful, whimsical artwork for the young and young at heart. Her projects range from invitations and tote bags to coloring books and kids' apps. Visit hollydoodlestudio.com for more examples of Holly's work and custom illustration. **(pages 40–41, 100, 142, 170)**

Lori Danelle Wilson—letterer and illustrator—has been filling sketchbooks since childhood. A lifelong creative, she daydreams about what could be and stays up half the night to make it happen. Working with her husband, Lori co-owns **Home Again Creative**, offering paper and home goods, thoughtfully crafted to bring you whimsy and joy. **(pages 8–9, 51, 84, 109, 187)**

Zachary Horst is a graphic designer and artist living just north of Austin in Georgetown, Texas, with his husband, Taylor, and their cat, Cy. He loves color and form and is always working on some new project. **(pages 10, 90, 104–105, 155)**

Carol Jarvis, from Chicago, studied printmaking and painting at Barat College in Illinois and the Art Institute of Chicago. Carol is a contributor for the Phantom Hand artist group in Philadelphia. Her commercial paintings have been showcased from coast to coast in the United States and in Canada. **(pages 68, 110, 148, 200–201)**

Joel and Ashley Illustration are a husband-and-wife team who met in a freshman drawing class and hit it off during a fabric study. They run a freelance studio and paper goods company, This Paper Ship, from their home in Sanford, North Carolina, which they share with their daughter, four cats, antique letterpress, and piles of laundry. You can find them online at joelandashleyillustration.com. **(pages 14, 96–97, 131, 158)**

Caitlin Keegan is an illustrator and pattern designer based in Brooklyn. She is the creator of *The Illuminated Tarot: 53 Cards for Divination and Gameplay*, published in 2017. Caitlin is a graduate of the Rhode Island School of Design. To see more of Caitlin's work, visit caitlinkeegan.com. **(pages 29, 58, 163, 176–177)**

Jen Keenan is an illustrator and designer located in Brooklyn. She strives to create pieces of art that capture a sort of childlike whimsy. Her illustrative work celebrates hand-drawn imperfections, lettering, and quirky sophistication. Her work may be found at jenkeenan.com. **(pages 24–25, 52, 141, 192)**

South Florida artist Megan Wells, the artist behind **Makewells**, is inspired by beautiful words and God's natural wonders. Her work combines whimsical florals with flowing letterforms. When not busy creating in her studio, you can find her riding her bike to the beach with her husband, Brent, and lovable min-pin, George. **(pages 4, 56–57, 87, 183)**

João Neves is a graphic designer and illustrator from Lisbon, Portugal. He's mostly known for his lettering work, the fruit of his obsession with vintage graphic design and typography. Some of the clients he has worked for include Disney, Vodafone, and DC Shoes. His projects range from branding and T-shirt designs to painting skateboards and murals. **(pages 94, 128–129, 179, 197)**

Rae Ritchie is an illustrator and pattern surface designer based in Minneapolis, Minnesota. Rae's work, focused on flowers, ferns, and star-filled skies, captures the magic and wonder in the everyday. Painted in a sunny room in her home, these gouache creations are licensed for product development in the fabric, publishing, and home decor industries. **(pages 7, 35, 144–145, 173, 188)**

Gemma Román is a Mexican illustrator and letterer. Inspired by the colors of her land, her work has been published in magazines from the US and the UK. She illustrates children's books for different countries and her art has been part of exhibitions in California, New York, and México. **(pages 7, 125–126, 152–153)**

Clair Rossiter is a freelance illustrator working just outside of London. She graduated from Falmouth University in 2014, and primarily uses gouache, pencils, and digital techniques to create her illustrations. Pop over to clairrossiter.com if you would like to see a little more of Clair's work. **(pages 19, 74, 112–113, 191)**

Beth Rufener is a graphic designer and hand-letterer living in northeastern Ohio with her husband and two children. Scripture is her favorite artistic subject, and her art draws inspiration from the rich illumination, ornaments, and flourishing from centuries past. See more of her lettering at instagram.com/creatifolio. **(pages 36, 71, 116, 136–137)**

Angela Southern is a lettering artist from the Midwest, currently living in Austin, Texas. Her work has been recognized by *Communication Arts Magazine* and the Type Directors Club. A few of her clients include the *Wall Street Journal*, Converse, *Time Out New York*, and the *Ritz-Carlton Magazine*. **(pages 16–17, 45, 83, 174)**

EJTee, or EJ, for short,is a hand-lettering artist from Singapore. His style of lettering varies from brush to centuries-old roman capitals. He loves to use black ink in his work for its high contrast and impact. A perfectionist, he is always finding ways to improve his skill. You can follow his work on Instagram @ewejintee or at ejtee.com **(pages 67, 77, 138, 194–195)**

Wendy Xu is a letterer and illustrator based in Los Angeles. Her passion for letterforms has led her to explore a variety of styles, from calligraphic expressions and digital type to illustrative lettering. Her work has been recognized by the Type Directors Club with the Certificate of Typographic Excellence. **(pages 42, 99, 132, 184–185)**

A WORD OF EXPLANATION

Many contemporary translations of the Bible do not capitalize pronouns such as "he" and "him," because these words were not capitalized in the original Greek and Hebrew texts. While many of us think that capital letters show reverence for God, the translators opted for fidelity to the original usage. We have decided to remain true to the translation with regard to capitalization, as well as other grammar and punctuation.